THE NAKED TRUTH
By Tamika Melvin

Royalty Crowned Publishing
Raleigh, NC
www.royaltycrownedpub.com
ISBN 13: 978-1-7371592-1-6
Copyright: 1-10470345151
LCCN Library Congress:
Cover Design: Tori Mckoy
Cover Photo: Tori Mckoy
Interior Design: Lissha Sadler
Edited By: Megan Joseph, for Joseph Editorial Services
Proofreading: Megan Joseph and Tamika Melvin
Copyright@2021 by Tamika Melvin

All rights are reserved. In accordance with the U.S. Copyright Act of 1976, the scanning, uploading, and electronic sharing of any part of this book without the permission of the publisher constitute unlawful piracy and theft of the author's intellectual property. No part of this book may be reproduced in any manner whatsoever without written permission, except in the case of brief quotations embodied in critical articles and reviews.

First of all, I want to give all praises to the most high for guiding my path and protecting against the enemies traps. God is the alpha and omega I'm forever grateful for fully letting you lead my life.

DEDICATION

This book is dedicated to my mother Angela Melvin Freeman, Father Alexander McEachin and my grandparents Charles and Virginia Edwards continue to SIP my angels.

I am also dedicating this to my Aunt Diana and Uncle Ronnie. I miss you both terribly thanks for being major influences in my life.

To my three KINGS: Shaimek, Shacory and Sharhon Williams, Mommy will forever teach y'all perseverance, consistency, survival, strength, and most of all resilience. I will not let y'all subject yourselves to be a product of your environment but the rise of breaking generational transfer. I am going to forever instill spiritual guidance as well as good morals into each of you.

I want to say thanks to all my family and friends. I love you all so very much. I'm grateful for all the lessons that turned out to be blessings.

The Naked Truth (Remember My Name)
A Tale of Resilience, Grit, Strength and Courage.

Tamika Melvin

Chapter 1

Not Easily Broken –
♥ ♥ ♥ Brooklyn, Where My Story Began ♥ ♥ ♥

I grew up in the Brownsville section of Brooklyn, New York from birth to the early 1990s. Growing up in that era, I encountered a lot in my household and in the streets. By the time I was six-years-old, me, my mother and her boyfriend along with my little sister moved to Sally Matthew's apartment complex, which is now called Brownsville Gardens or Sallies, that was built in the early 1980s. I can still remember growing up there like it was yesterday.

Growing up we played games like skelly, red light green light, tag, hide and seek, double Dutch, steal the bacon, coco-levio, hopscotch, red rover, hand ball, Simon says, and video games like Atari and Nintendo. I would go across the street from my building to Berto Store for goodies on the corner Legion Street and Pitkin Avenue.

Sometimes we would walk up Pitkin Avenue to shop and eat. As we walked the block, we could hear music blaring from the stores or from cars that were up and down the strip. I still remember the aroma of the orange Spanish food truck that sat on Pitkin. New York is very diverse so it's nothing to find international foods there.

Everyone on the block was like family. Yeah of course we had our share of disagreements and fights, but no matter what we stuck together. In our neighborhood we really lived by it takes a village because you were disciplined by whatever adult caught you doing something wrong. Sallies wasn't the projects, but it was low-income housing that helped many low-income welfare dependent families. I remember growing up on the paper food stamps, welfare cheese, powdered milk and no-frills products. I was very lucky to have a family full of cooks, both male and female.

The Naked Truth

Living in Sallies, nobody could come over there messing with us and not have a fight on their hands. I remember all the fun I had growing up, but I also recall the not so fun times too.

Around 1985 in Brownsville, I saw a guy who was stabbed and died right on the sidewalk a few feet from my building. I still can remember how his grandmother screamed when the ambulance couldn't revive him. I was seven years old but I still remember my mother, aunt and neighbor all tried to keep him talking but it was too late.

Another time when me and some of my friends were playing double Dutch outside, a guy ran by, dropped some money and asked us to pick it up. About five minutes later, the man who was chasing him ran by us with a gun in his hand. That was so scary to actually see but it definitely wasn't the last time I saw a gun.

There was also a time on Lott Avenue, a block where some of my family lived, that I witnessed my Nana being shot at by my aunt's boyfriend at the time. The asshole didn't even care that me, my sister, and cousins were standing right there. He shot at her in front of us. I remember sitting in the car with my Nana, mother, and aunt, then the trigger-happy asshole appeared and I told my Nana and mom. Next thing I knew, my uncle Ron appeared and beat his tail. I was so glad because he could have hurt or killed Nana.

Sad to say but that wasn't the end of me seeing acts of violence at all. As a matter of fact, I saw a lot more the older I got. Most kids probably just saw things like that on television but I actually lived it.

In the 1980s the crack epidemic hit New York big time. The inner-city low-income areas were impacted the most. Growing up during that time I saw a lot of crimes being committed, children in foster homes, violent behavior and many deaths due to this drug. Even though crack wasn't in my household directly, I still came in close contact with it daily. We had neighbors who indulged in it so we would smell it in the hallways of the buildings in Sallies. That is a smell that is distinctive and one I will never forget.

Tamika Melvin

As children we played outside a lot, so we would see crack vials on the ground with different color caps. The poor neighborhoods were being torn apart by the crack epidemic. Once people began using, they became desperate, willing to do anything to get another hit because the high was very short-lived. You would see people doing anything to have that high from robbing and stealing, prostitution, selling their children, and/or even killing someone. That drug was powerful and it tore apart many black and brown families. I never had to experience it with my mother but I did come in contact with people who did. It was heartbreaking to watch someone who was on drugs basically sell their soul, but it was even worse to see people having to deal with a family member on it.

Growing up I didn't realize that my siblings, cousins, and I were exposed to the most unsafe environments as children. We were in the presence of people who indulged in drugs, alcohol, and acts of crime and violence. I remember we would visit two buildings, 43 and 45 on Lott Avenue, the block I mentioned earlier located in Brownsville. Those buildings reminded me of The Carter buildings that was in the movie New Jack City that came out in 1991. I would see people go knock on a door and buy crack as the dealer serve it through the keyhole. The fiends would be shooting up and smoking crack in the hallways. This was something I saw on a regular. I can still remember how gritty it was and the terrible smell. We would also go to Langston Hughes projects to visit family where we would see the same things happening. Oh, let me not forget the urine smell in hallways, elevators, and stairways. The stairways are where you would sometimes see people getting high, drunk, or even sleeping. This was in the 80s and early 90s era so the parties, violence and drugs were big up north back then.

There were a few times when my family had card games or parties that would get out of hand. I saw my oldest brother's dad stab one of my aunt's boyfriends over gambling. I saw people get shot and shot at, stabbed, badly beaten, hit with bottles and many other acts of violence was around me because of gambling. Growing up in Brooklyn during those times was definitely an experience, but I don't regret any of it because it taught me survival, courage and how to be fearless.

The purpose of this heart tugging story is to prove that through obstacles you can make it through anything, as long as you keep God (or whoever you pray to) first in your life. This is not to belittle my family or my upbringing but to simply bring awareness of how to break learned behavior. You can do what your heart desires as long as you stop the repetition of bad habits and behavior.

You all will take this mental journey with me to places I thought I would never speak about again. Although it was emotionally draining, my past helped me learn to be my true self and unapologetically happy. Yeah, these are all true events I will speak on. I actually was advised from my therapist a lot of my anxiety and aggression stemmed from things I've encountered growing up. I thank you God for my ability to be resilient and open.

❤ ❤ ❤ Mommy's Keeper ❤ ❤ ❤

I encountered abuse early on in my life from the age of six years old to ten-years-old. I watched my mom go through abuse at the hands of my stepdad. The first time I saw my mother get struck by a man is a feeling I will never forget. It was a beautiful sunny day and we were walking toward King's Highway when my mom saw one of her cousin's boyfriends, who greeted her with a hug and kiss on the cheek. I saw the rage in my stepdad's face instantly, but my mom continued her conversation with the man.

After saying goodbye, we began to walk towards 98th Street and Rutland Road. My stepdad started cursing at my mom about the guy kissing her on the cheek. In addition to them arguing, he hauled off and smacked the hell out of her, which startled me and my little sister. He told us to be quiet and we just walked back home in silence. I couldn't have been more than six or seven years old, but I still recall how I felt in that moment.

It was like after that day all I can remember is him hitting my mom a lot and being very disrespectful to us, especially me. There was a time I saw them fighting over a rifle that my mom pulled on him after being fed up with him hitting her. However, I guess she wasn't fed up enough, because when everything died down, he still was there in the house. The beatings just got worse and I became even more scared for my mother's life. She had to sneak to drink her beer, she couldn't have too many male friends, and he didn't like when our family was visiting. He was just a very controlling man who I grew to despise.

I expressed to my nana and my uncle Ron how I didn't want to be there, but I always missed my mom and my siblings. After a while, I would beg my Nana to take me back home and regretted it every time I went back. I just wanted to be there so I can defend my mother. At the age of eight-years-old, I felt like I had to make sure she was okay.

I would hide things I think he would use to hurt or even kill her, such as knives and sticks. Anything that I felt he would use to hurt her. I would write notes saying I hate you or I hope you die and leave them in the bathroom and he would go tell my mother I was disrespectful, and I needed my tail whipped. Hell, I didn't care I wanted to hurt him like I felt he was hurting my mommy.

One particular day they were fighting, and I yelled, "I HATE YOU!" to him and he turned to me like always, but I didn't give a damn. I was getting more afraid for my mom's life at this point. He smacked me down to the floor and kicked me a few times, cursing at me. I was yelling mean things at him still balled up on the floor until he picked up a chair. Mind you, I'm like eight or nine years old at this point.

I remember looking in the doorway of my bedroom seeing my mom and she yelled "No!" and ran in her room. I felt so hurt because I wanted my mommy to protect me but instead, she ran off. Not because she was scared, she was trying to turn his attention to her. I can tell you one thing, from that day forward, the rage in me began.

I really started to look at my mom in a terrible light because I couldn't understand why she would continue being with a man that fought and bruised her. I would be embarrassed because I would catch our neighbors talking about it in our building or sitting on the stoup. It even got to a point where my mom's best friend jumped in one of the fights with them. I remember being over my brother's godmother's house next door and my mom's best friend knocking on the door to let us know she was okay. She told my brother's god mother, "She stupid," and that stuck with me. I started thinking like is my mom really stupid? It didn't matter though, the fights got worse and she eventually ended up getting the police involved and making him move out the apartment.

    She had finally started putting more time in us and I felt a whole lot better about sleeping at night. Although everything seemed like it was going in a better route, my mom started drinking more and I knew she missed him. She had to take care of three kids along with her sister's two kids a male and female. My oldest auntie was going through her own trials so yes it probably was a lot on her without his help financially. I just remember feeling so much more at peace and not so stressed as a nine-year-old child. Eventually my stepdad worked his way back into her good graces and it didn't take long before she was back under his spell. My mom was sneaking talking to him on the phone, going to see him and spending nights at his place. She was doing a good job keeping it from our family, but they weren't stupid. Especially my mom's two sisters.

    I remember my older female cousin that lived with us had a little boy. I was so happy I loved that baby so much from the day he entered this earth. She is more like our big sister because she looked out for me, my sister, and brother a lot. Although my family wasn't too thrilled, they pulled together to give a nice baby shower for her. My stepdad was in attendance and didn't seem too happy. My mom had a lot of company he didn't know or approve of, but he knew not to start any shit that night.

    See I always watched his actions when other men or even other people were around, he didn't even know how much I watched him. His controlling behavior was hidden from others, but I was always on to his mess. After the shower was over, I heard my mom telling one of her girlfriends she asked him to leave because he was upset. I do remember him leaving and that was a night I didn't have to hear my mom scream.

The last memory I will always have of my mom being in that situation was when my stepdad was in the hospital. I can still recall her sitting us down and telling us he was coming home. She went on to say they were getting married and if we didn't like it, I could go stay with my Nana and my sister could go with her godmother. I never really understood how much my mother loved him until I got older. At that moment is when I realized that no matter how much he hurt her, she would never leave him. I was heartbroken but I loved my mommy and just wanted her to be happy.

Unfortunately, before he could make it out the hospital he passed away. I remember on May 14th, 1988, me and my best friend were having our birthday party together her mom threw us. Everything was going great and all of the sudden I heard a scream from mommy that let me know something was wrong. My first thought was my stepdad didn't make it but I wasn't sure, so I went next door to our apartment to see what was wrong. There my mom was crying, and everyone was trying to console her because just as I thought my stepdad had passed away.

At that point I felt so bad for her and my oldest brother, but I was relieved at the same time. I felt like if he made it back in the house my mom would probably end up dead like one of her friends did years earlier. It was hell as a child to have to worry that your mother may be killed by the hands of her boyfriend. I thought the days of terror had ended once he passed, but I was wrong. We encountered more chaos in the next couple of years. Now I can truly understand why they say children follow what they see because I did.

My mom was heartbroken and drinking very heavy. She started trying to mend her heart but instead encountered more anguish in the years to come. She went back to my biological father which didn't work out. From what I hear he was doing hard drugs and wasting money so that didn't last long.

The Naked Truth

What's the point in being around if you're not there to help the situation? Truth be told, I wasn't really thrilled at all about him being around. I didn't know him and he didn't try to get to know me. I think it was over after a few months and so was my relationship with him at that time.

Then she went back to my sister's father who I loved and really knew as Daddy. That was also short lived because he ended up with one of his ex-girlfriend's and it happened right under my mother's nose. All I heard was the woman was invited to my mom's house, later down the line a party happened he helped give, my mom found out and it was over between them. Long story short heartbreak had struck again.

She later met my second brother's father through her neighbor who was also her best friend I spoke of earlier. He was a big, tall dude, like football player big. He was also very abusive to my mother, a con artist and a freaking thief. My brother was born in May 1990 prematurely due to abuse and stress.

At this point, I had gotten older and was so full of rage. So, whenever they fought, damn right I got in it. I felt like I was older now and wasn't letting my mother get beat in front of me no more. I would pick up whatever was in sight and hit his ass with it: bats, sticks, brooms, anything that was around. My boy cousin who also lived with us even jumped on his ass. This dude was sneaky with his shit though he would fight her mostly when no one was around. He went as far as stealing my baby brother's baby shower gifts and burning my mother with cigarettes in her sleep. He was a full-blown coward. I started to despise him the way I once felt about my first brother's father. My family would come over there to kick his butt but of course my mom turned against them. Why? Because she was in love. I felt like if something didn't give my family would hurt him really bad or eventually kill him.

When my mom decided to move to North Carolina I didn't want to go. I was angry about it because my mother cried so bad, but I felt like if she didn't leave New York my second brother's dad would have killed her.

Tamika Melvin

Drugs were flooding the streets and crime was high. She felt she needed to leave New York to save herself and her children because it was getting worse by the day. My baby aunt and oldest uncle were already in Raleigh, North Carolina so it seemed like the perfect plan.

However, we didn't end up in Raleigh, we moved to Chapel Hill to a shelter and that's where we met our extended family. We have contact with people from there until this day. My family felt it was a good idea for her to go to the shelter to get help. I just never understood why they would be okay with us being in a place with strangers. Why people didn't pull together to help their family but let them go to shelters. I know we were supposed to stay with my baby aunt but it only lasted a short time. Until this day it has been several stories said as to why we couldn't live with her but it was a blessing in that lesson for my mom. We lived in a shelter that was very strict with rules. We got up at six a.m. for breakfast and dinner was served at six p.m. I was teased and bullied in middle school for living in a shelter and had to protect myself by any means. My mom hated it but she did everything she could to make sure we were alright. She protected us best she knew how like any mother would. She snuck us food when we were hungry and tried her best to get us what we needed. We missed curfew, got caught eating after dinner a couple of times, and my mom was warned about alcohol on her breath. I knew she was drinking when she could to cope with this situation. The shelter had a three-strike policy and they would put you out. Well, my mom hit those three strikes and we were put out. I mean all our belongings were on the streets and she was so hurt and embarrassed.

We eventually met a family who later became my mom's in laws who took us in after getting put out with all our stuff from the shelter and that's how my mother met my third brother's father. I went to live with a teacher's aide from my middle school for a while until my mother got her own place. Eventually, the counselor tried to take me from my mother and tried to encourage me to speak against her but that wasn't happening. I'm thankful for what she did for me but I wasn't leaving my mom. I loved my mom and wanted to be with her and my siblings. I will always love my current stepdad and his family because they took us in when we didn't have our own family. We struggled to adjust and my mom worked her way up to get us our own place.

For a small time, while my mom and my stepdad went back and forth with their relationship, she let my second brother's dad move down south with us about a year after we were there. I was angry because she did it while Nana was visiting from New York, which made her so upset she left Chapel Hill. I couldn't understand why she would want a man who hits her, but the stay didn't last long. He was back doing drugs and stealing from stores which led to him being in the local paper. Me and my sister were embarrassed because Chapel Hill is a small town, so everyone knew it was him because our address was in the paper. He was a sorry ass dude but my mom loved him for some reason.

One day, me and my homegirl were upstairs talking and we heard my mother yell out, so we ran downstairs to see that they had gotten into it. Me and my friend jumped in his face but of course my mom wouldn't say anything. You know that arrangement was short lived, and I thank God she woke up quickly.

She eventually started to seriously date my youngest brother's father and we became a family. Nope, I wasn't thrilled in the beginning because he was about twelve years younger than her, but he loved her and that eventually became enough for us.

He didn't have any kids but took us in as his own and treated us better than anyone else she had ever been with. I will forever love him for that and although they are no longer together, he has never treated us bad or stopped loving us or her.

John 15:4-5: Remain in me, as I also remain in you. No branch can bear fruit by itself; it must remain in the vine. Neither can you bear fruit unless you remain in me. I am the vine; you are the branches. If you remain in me and I in you, you will bear much fruit; apart from me you can do nothing.

Chapter 2

Generational Transfer-
♥ ♥ ♥ Repetition of Negative Behavior ♥ ♥ ♥

My family was raised on welfare but built on hustle. We were taught to do what we have to do to take care of our children. I remember living in Brooklyn my mom doing many things to make ends meet from babysitting, to selling weed, to selling plates at her rent parties and card games. My mother did what she had to do to make sure her children had a roof over their head and a meal every day. Yes, mistakes were made just like that of any parent, but she did her best. She grew up in a certain environment where partying was acceptable every day of the week. Therefore, she repeated the same cycle in her household as well.

Back in the day, whether it was a birthday, anniversary, baby shower, card game, or just a get together, it was always a party when my family came together. The gatherings were mostly at my family or their close friends' houses. The kids were fed and sent in the room, while the adults drank, danced, smoked and blasted music to the wee hours of the morning. The aroma of fried chicken, weed and cigarettes filled the air. As I look back at those days, it made me realize the love and togetherness my family shared. However, in addition to all the great times we shared, there was also some unpleasant times as well.

I would like to openly say, despite how close we are, there were times when we were at each other's throats. When my mom would go through her domestic disputes, my Nana came over to our house ready to whip ass. She didn't care how bad those men thought they were, she would shoot a bastard quick. Nobody was putting hands on her children and getting away with it. Nana was not to be messed with and people around Brooklyn knew better. You definitely couldn't bother her family or she was coming for you right or wrong.

The Naked Truth

I would call her collect every time my mom fought with those men. I knew Mommy would be mad but I always let Nana know what was going on. That's one thing I can say, I never saw Nana let a man hit her. I always would see her being the aggressor and would think to myself, I'm going to be like my nana.

I never had respect for a man who put his hands on a woman. I was so confused on how a woman can love a man so much that she can deal with physical abuse. I later learned when vulnerability kicked in, I was no different than my mom. I dealt with physical abuse later on in life because I was pushed in a corner.

See when I dealt with my physical abuse, it was months after losing my mother and Nana. That for me was like losing two mothers and they were the only people I could really talk to family wise. The time I needed my family the most, we were slowly dividing. At that point is when I knew I had to fully depend and lean on God. I tried to escape an abusive, drug addicted person but I didn't really have the support I needed. At the time, my own people weren't trustworthy so I had to turn to friends.

I'm not bashing anyone but at that time I needed people to have my back. I didn't need people to bash me and talk about me. I needed love, support, and encouragement but like I said my family had some not so good times which led my nana to her death. I will speak on that later in this journey.

My family is close nit but we are also very dysfunctional at times. I can say all the generations from my great-grandmother down to the one after me, are a little detached from reality. The repetition of habits and behavior that engulfed my bloodline has somewhat hindered our spiritual growth. Engaging in drinking, smoking, partying, arguing, fighting, doing and selling drugs was what I knew growing up. I didn't know the presence of God and how important it is to have a relationship with him. I didn't have any solid people in my family to lead me in that spiritual direction. North Carolina is known as a Bible state, so I was embarrassed when I didn't know more about the common scriptures and gospel music. When I was growing up, we didn't follow any religious practices in our household. I learned about God later on in my life from research, friends and joining several churches. My nana did take me to church here and there when I was younger but it was not consistent.

I learned how to be a parent through my upbringing. Was it all good? No! There were many trials I went through to finally see that I had to make a change. I found myself putting my kids through the same bull shit I went through as a child. I talked all that junk about how I grew up but repeated the same habits with my own children. I was fixated on living the same life I witnessed growing up. I really couldn't wait to grow up so I could party all night. That is all I knew was partying, drinking, smoking, and blasting music all night.

It seemed I was fixated on living the same traumatic life I came up in. I had shootouts at my first two apartments behind beef my older male cousin had with some dudes. I had people smoking weed and selling drugs around my children. They saw their dad get arrested a few times and even me get roughed up by police. Basically, I ended up having my kids around the same type of environment I was in when I was growing up. I thought that kind of stuff I did was cool in my twenties and thirties. Getting high everyday with people in and out my house around my kids was at one point an everyday move. Although most of the time it was family, that didn't mean craziness didn't pop off.

My kids' father sold drugs out the house where one time the police picked him up. I allowed it because it was fast money and helped with the bills in the house. My ex-husband had a felony background so his jobs didn't pay well. It didn't help that he didn't have the best work ethic so we stayed in constant binds. There were many times when we were homeless because of his inability to hold down a job. I would have to pay the bills alone and many times couldn't handle it. We would argue and fight because he wasn't coming home, cheating, getting locked up and not holding down his jobs.

I realized he just wasn't ready for a family and I didn't know how to move on and accept it. I saw my mother try to see the good in men that weren't shit and that was her biggest downfall. I realized I was doing the same thing but when I did, I was four kids in. No matter how much I wanted to see the good in him, he just wasn't ready to be a family man. I accepted infidelity on numerous occasions and continued having kids by someone I should have left many years ago. I repeated the same cycle with my relationships that I saw the women in my family deal with. They stayed with men who didn't respect them like they deserved.

I grew up with my nana having a boyfriend during her marriage most of my life. As much as I use to think it was cool that she was able to do that, I later learned that it was morally and spiritually wrong. Not saying I don't understand why she did it, but it definitely wasn't right, especially for her grandchildren to see. I knew what to say around my grandad and not to mention the other man. We would be gone for the whole weekend and my grandfather never questioned it. I was always confused on why he didn't care where we were. The weekdays we spent home and she would do her wifely duties. Then the weekends we were gone to her boyfriend's house. That was our schedule for years and I was used to it.

She always explained to me that once my grandfather cheated on her she never trusted him again. I always wondered why she stayed with him if he cheated when she could have moved on. The women back then stuck it out with their husbands because most of the time they were the breadwinners. As a little girl, I didn't really see women going to work like that. Most of the women I was around worked odd jobs, on welfare and were homemakers. I didn't see too many women in the corporate world, except those on television.

I remember watching a show in the eighties named Dynasty with Linda Evans as Krystle, Joan Collins as Alexis, and Diahann Carroll as Dominque. I would always mimic them putting on my nana's wigs and custom jewelry acting and writing out the parts. I would think of how one day I wanted to get a job where I have to wear business suits. I dreamed of dressing up to go to fancy events and drinking wine. I will say I experienced some of those things and I'm still trying to do so much more. Repeating those same behaviors put me so far behind with my life plan but as you read on you will become inspired. My nana and mommy had their flaws as we all do but they also showed me how to be an awesome cook, a fighter, hustler, dainty, and most of all respectful.

 Facts of Life

My siblings and I later endured and displayed verbal, physical, and emotional abuse in our own relationships. That was because of what we saw and heard within our surroundings. We weren't given the tools as adults to know how to properly raise our children, be spouses, or even stop the generational curses. I will tell you this, all of it was a valuable lesson and we vowed to try our best to do better with our children in the future. I don't blame my family because what we all endured was from learned behaviors. I made a lot of mistakes in my life, but I can say today I'm learning to right my wrongs and be a better woman and mother to my sons. I will speak my truth because I can and I'm not ashamed of it. Family I love you, but I will speak my peace.

As a little girl I always yearned for the love of my father. I wanted so much to have a relationship with my biological dad when I became a teenager. Instead, I got men who tried their best to play the role however it wasn't the same. Through research, writing letters, and social media I finally found my dad August 2016. I thank God that I did because now that missing piece of my puzzle is now filled. He was not in the best health because he had a stroke and was in a nursing home. I just thank God that I was able to find him alive because I ended up losing him at the end of 2020. The sad part about it is I tried to see him on December 19th, 2020, and no one told me he died days before on December 15th. No one even tried to contact me so I found out through Facebook. I'm thankful however that I found him so now that chapter of my life is closed. I still don't have a sense of my identity from my dad side of the family but I did connect to my half-brother and a couple of aunts. We all are currently navigating through trying to have a relationship. I guess it will happen in its own timing. I was angry with my father for years but after seeing him in that vulnerable state smiling it warmed even the coldest part of my heart for him.

I later learned that my mom grew up in a broken household and used the parenting tools that she was shown. How do I know? I'm now a woman and mother too. I know how it is to love a man so much that you may neglect your responsibilities as a mother. I let men manipulate my mind and rob me of my time. I should have been spending way more time with my children. I dealt with a lot emotional and mental abuse which is just as bad as physical abuse. I'm not going to say no man ever put their hands on me because one coward ass bastard did. However, it didn't go on for years or even months, and best believe it was not an easy task trying to go against me. I am my grandmother's child, after all. I encountered abuse and I swore to never let it happen again. My kids weren't around during that time because he probably would be dead. I can't believe I even dealt with a sorry bastard like that. It makes me cringe.

My mom always let it be known that she dealt with abuse and disrespect but she never wanted her girls to deal with it. Me and my sister thought because we weren't getting beat, we were in better situations. Well, we were wrong disrespect and verbal abuse can break you down mentally. Men will tear you down until you feel so low you have nothing to give to anyone, not even your children. I would see my mom so sad some days because when she loved she love hard. When her marriage ended, I saw how much that took out of her. She dated after but she became so dependent on her children and my nana that she didn't know how to give to another relationship. I was so determined not to be that way. After my marriage ended, I isolated myself too much and didn't know how to open up to anyone. Growing up with so much confusion going on around me forced me to be a hidden basket case. I became vulnerable at an early age and forced myself to grow up fast and became a mom when I wasn't ready.

The Naked Truth

My siblings and I were never really encouraged about education and future plans like we should have been. I'm not saying my mom didn't care she just didn't force us to do things that we didn't want to do. Three out of five of us have a high school diploma and two of us attended college. Now that I'm in my forties I see that getting an education and living life was way more important. I went on my own before I was ready to do so which made me a product of my environment. We thought having children, getting married, and having our own apartments was what life was about.

We didn't plan our future so we could live comfortably and grow as adults. As a matter of fact, everything we did was for the moment and no advancement was really done. We all have children, besides my youngest brother, and vowed to show them a different way of life. I don't think we learned who we were coming up into adulthood. I want our children to put their education first and know what they want out of life.

They need to travel and experience all life has to offer. I don't want my sons to miss out on opportunities that could help them grow as men and have a brighter future. I need them to be better than me and their father. I want them to always get along with each other and their cousins. It's sad to say but the older women in my family brought on the envy and strife amongst us.

My nana left here broken hearted with us in complete chaos and turmoil. There was never a resolution completed for us to communicate better as a family. We kiss and hug each other every time we encounter one another, but what is that when the love isn't genuine. To me that is being fake and showing a façade of togetherness when that isn't the case at all.

I've tried on many occasions to mend broken fences and extend olive branches with certain family members but it just doesn't work. I had to focus on my growth to be a better woman and mother to my children. I had to live for me because tomorrow isn't promised. I know that I'm most important and when people can walk away from me let them walk. It's most hurtful when the people you look to for love won't show it, but what you do find is envy and betrayal. You can't get rid of family but you can choose how you deal with them.

❤ ❤ ❤ Unlearning Learned Behavior ❤ ❤ ❤

When I finally decided to seek therapy, it was in 2018, I was turning forty years old that year and my life needed a change. People didn't know I carried around so much hurt, anger, and resentment that I wanted to kill myself.

On several occasions over the years, I felt like my own relatives hated me. I felt alone and dealt with everything from molestation, physical abuse, rape, my child's death, domestic abuse and a failed marriage. Each of those situations I dealt with completely alone. I didn't have people checking in on me or comforting me. I found comfort through drinking and getting high. Yes, everyone has dealt with tragic things in their life but I needed my family and I didn't have that.

I put all the anguish I felt in my writing and tried to build my own empire. In doing so, I released two books, a magazine, my own lip gloss, and a nightwear and bedroom candy line. So why wouldn't my own people want to see me flourish? I will never know.

When I turned forty-years-old I said to myself, "Forget this I didn't do anything wrong. I'm tired of chasing relationships with my family." If they don't appreciate or want my love, I will give it to the ones that do and that's exactly what I'm doing.

My spiritual sister once told me, "Tamika you have a mean streak, you're very bitter and definitely not approachable, which means you're not perfect, but you did nothing wrong but be born. You didn't ask to be light skin, have light brown eyes, or to be your grandmother's favorite. Life just happened that way and now you are suffering the consequences of life. You're the Joseph of your family. You will be the one who show your family that spirituality is important." In reading the stories of Joseph he was a dreamer and conqueror who never gave up. I now understand what she tried to tell me. Joseph was envied, assaulted and enslaved but God chose him to preserve his family.

I finally decided to live for me and my children. Life became easier once I started to weed out the negative aspects and focus on my household. I had to let so many situations from my past go, because the pain I harbored had me in a depressed mindset. If I wanted to have peace in my future, I had to find a way to deal with my past. Admitting that I had issues was the first step in the right direction. Being broken inside wasn't hurting anybody but my children and I, so I had to do some serious damage control.

I begin therapy again in 2020 after stopping in 2019 and it was the best thing I could have ever done. Breaking the generational transfers became so much more important to me during this most memorable year.

I lost my mother and nana in 2019, which I definitely wasn't ready for. Instead of letting the grief consume me, I put that energy into renewing myself spiritually and mentally. Oh, don't get it twisted I did self-medicate for a little while but I quickly pulled it together. I was going in a downward spiral and no one could save me but me.

Losing them was detrimental for my family as a whole because during both times we weren't a united front like we needed to be. We appeared as this close nit and loving family that sticks together at all times but that was far from the truth. We are just as dysfunctional as many other families, maybe a little bit more if you asked me.

In my family, we tend to seek acceptance from the outside world more than we do with each other. I saw so much backstabbing and underhanded mess go on in my family that most times I'd just rather keep my distance than be around it. I have had so many people tell me how my own family has said I act bougie. I'm mean, I do think I'm bad. How they only dealt with me because I'm family, and the list goes on.

These are things I heard from their own peers who felt the need to inform me of what was being said but that's nothing new, I'm used to it. I learned to not let that nonsense bother me anymore. I just let it roll off my shoulders and keep my distance. Negative energy has no place in my life. This is why I blame the generations before us because things like this were made to be okay. I will never indulge in my sons talking about their own family or let them feel it's okay. It's definitely not good to discuss grown up business in front of your children and I know that went on a lot in my family.

People don't understand in doing that you make children draw their own conclusions about people at a young age. My children can never say I told them anything about the adults in my family. That's definitely a generational transfer I see that still goes on and with my sons I will not have it. To me that just leaves the door open for them to be disrespectful and create opinions of people older than them that they shouldn't.

Hell, my friends can't say I came to them just talking crap about my family unless someone came and told me something first. I never found joy in talking junk about my family unless something was brought to me. Many times, I came to friends because I was hurt behind things that were said or how I was being treated. It's been many times I've heard things from them like, "Girl I would have been cut them off, "or "How can you deal with them, family or not?"

As I said in the last section, you can't rid yourself of family but learn how to deal with them. I unlearned being angry and learned that distance is the best line of protection for my peace of mind. To keep my sanity, I no longer listened to the bones people carried to me about what was said about me. At the end of the day, if I keep coming up in conversations, I definitely must be important and envied a lot. I learned to stay silent and let God deal with those people. It takes way too much energy to be mad at people.

Another trait I will break with my sons is letting it be okay to bring different mates around me. I know you can't make anyone be with someone they're not happy with but I won't be dealing with several at one time. My motto is: if you ain't ready to settle down, then don't bring them around. I don't want to build a relationship with Lisa today and then they bring Monica next week (fictional names). I feel like it's disrespectful to the women and definitely to me as their mother. This is a trait I don't approve of that I grew up with in my family.

This is definitely something I saw firsthand and never really cared for. Like I said earlier for as long as I can remember my nana had a boyfriend and husband and this became normalized. How could we respect and have great morals about marriage if the matriarch of our family didn't show us that? My family may read this section and disagree with me putting certain things out there. However, this isn't to bash Nana in any way but to show the things that need to be broken within our family dynamic. This is simply to shine light on why we may have carried some of these generational curses to our children and mates. I've had my time of having my children around no-good men but I am righting my wrongs. This is something children should never see unless you're in a committed relationship. A child should never witness their parents in random relationships with seasonal people.

During my journey for change I had to break the need to be around people and partying cycle. Especially when that's all my children saw me do as they were growing up. I needed them to see me in a different light than what I saw growing up. I wanted them to see there's more to life than just drinking, smoking, getting high, selling drugs and blasting music to the wee hours of the morning. I had to show them there is fun without partying all the time and having a house full of people every day.

Playing games, vacations, going to the park, watching movies, arts and crafts, or just simply communicating what's going on with our lives can also be fun as a family. Don't get me wrong, I enjoyed every bit of the time I shared with my family because it made me the person that I am today. I just wish we had more activities and took trips together instead of always partying. I can't speak for others but I do want my boys to experience more than I did as far as traveling and experiences. I feel as a family if we traveled more, took vacations, and experience more things in life than just partying a lot of us would of went a lot further in life.

Tamika Melvin

I want us to acknowledge that a lot of toxicity came from the things we encountered from childhood. I want more for the generations after us and beyond. We can't continue to wallow in self-pity and blame the elder generations for our downfalls or mishaps. That should give us the boost we need to revamp our lives for the better.

I took the spiritual route to change my path in life and it's been the best thing I could have ever done for my sons and me. All I can say is thank God for guiding me to a path of healing because without him I wouldn't be nearly as focused, committed, bold, and forgiven as I am today. I'm forever thankful for his grace and mercy on my life because it could have been different. I really thought I was living life until I saw I wasn't. I was only existing like so many people are doing today. Take control of your destiny and unlearn the generational curses you're all so used to.

Prayer: God forgive us of all of these sins. Let your blood purify us from every sin that we have committed against you. Father God, purge every curse that has passed on in our family from generation to generation. In Jesus' name, I pray, Amen.

Chapter 3

Let's Do This Dirty Laundry-
♥ ♥ ♥Innocence Taken ♥ ♥ ♥

A dark time from my past that I remember, was when I was about seven-years old. My mom, me and my first-born brother who was an infant at the time walked up Pitkin Avenue to go see one of her long-time friends in Langston Hughes projects. I can recall her friend, asking her son, to keep me and my brother while they went out. We were all practically family, but what I encountered that night would become another part of my dark past.

There was a show called New York Hot Tracks that came on at nights many people use to watch. I can still smell the stench of Pine Sol and feel the cold drafty aura of the apartment located in the projects. My baby brother was only a few months old so he was asleep. My play cousin who was a teenager told me to get undressed so I can go to bed but then told me to sit on his lap. He began humping on me but of course at the time I really didn't understand what was going on. I guess he got bored with that because then he told me to get up, pulled out his penis, and told me to put it in my mouth. I was very sassy as a child so at first, I told him no.

He quickly popped me really hard on my arm and said it again, "Put it in your mouth and if you cry and wake up the baby, I'm going to whip your ass." As I type this, tears fill my eyes because I knew what he was doing was bad but I had no one there to save me. I did what he told me to do and to tell you the truth I still feel disgusted to this day. He forced my head down causing me to gag. I knew what he was doing was wrong but I just wanted it to all be over. The nasty bastard even masturbated right in front of me. Of course, I didn't understand what was going on but I remember him making noise and pulling on his penis very fast. To be seven-years-old and still remember the hurt, confusion, and violation I felt is nothing I can really put in words.

Tamika Melvin

I did eventually tell my nana who told my mother and they said they would handle it. My nana was furious when I told her. I do however remember one day hearing her saying to my mother that he was gay and she didn't see him doing that. She basically tried to say maybe it didn't really go down like I told them and it was never handled. That for me as a child made me lose a lot of trust in them.

Even at seven years old, nobody could convince me that I wasn't violated and forced to give oral sex. I know that I was humped and a penis was put in my mouth by a teenage boy my mother trusted to look after me and my little brother. His sexual orientation had nothing to do with what was done to me. He should have got his ass kicked, excuse my language, and put in jail.

As I got older, I learned several women in my family experienced the same thing or even worse sexual abuse. It was never discussed or handled like it should have been. Did this affect us when we became adults? Of course, it impacted our lives as women, mothers, and wives. After dealing with molestation, you can become sexually dissatisfied, extremely promiscuous, have low self-esteem, difficulty in relationships and heightened mental health issues. If you don't seek help and talk about this type of childhood trauma you can destroy yourself as a person.

I felt like if I couldn't depend on the women I loved so much, who could I run to? Dealing with sexual and physical abuse as a child brought on my own mental health issues. I learned that I have extreme anxiety, depression, and anger disorders. I went to get help because I knew something wasn't right with me. I will be the first to say that I will snap if pushed too far. I'm way better these days because I walk with God daily.

I can say that I no longer have resentment towards my mother for the past. We actually had the best bond because she accepted her faults and never made excuses. Like I said before, she played the hand she was dealt. Was it right? Hell no, but if you're not giving the right tools, how can you build something correctly? My mom read some of this book before she passed away. I thank God, she gave me the okay to speak my truth to help others.

So many people had their innocence taken as a child but only a few will talk about it. Children who are sexually or physically abused are usually threatened and fearful of the outcome if they said anything. Most abusers are usually related or close to their victims so it's hard for them to be exposed. You also have those families who would rather sweep shit under the rug then confront the situation. There were families that were good with not discussing this back in the days. However, all that does is continue to bring up more emotionally unstable women in the world.

Most of the time pedophiles are in denial about their behavior. Most don't even acknowledge that there is a problem and if they do, they don't care. I've come into close proximity with many who've been abused as a child, whether a female or male the distrust and anxiety remained the same.

The people who had hands in my abuse are now deceased. I was full of resentment, bitterness, and anger but once I truly forgave those who hurt me the blessings came so abundantly. I had to let go and forgive but the path isn't easy so I continue to be a work in progress. Healing starts with uprooting your past, releasing the hurt and anger, and cleansing your soul.

❤ ❤ ❤ The Fast and The Curious ❤ ❤ ❤

My curiosity grew about sex when I was around eleven-years-old. I was experimenting with girls and boys at this time. I didn't understand exactly what I was feeling or if I even liked it. People will deny these types of engagement but honey I was highly sexual with boys at twelve-years-old kissing, hugging, lost my virginity at fifteen. There were times when I would hump on pillows and touch myself even though I didn't know what masturbation was at the time. My mother saw I was getting fast and was on me hard. She thought leaving New York and going down south was the answer but boy was she wrong. I really got more access to be out and about. Not bragging but in North Carolina guys were driving at sixteen back then. I got into more mess than my mother could imagine.

The Naked Truth

Growing into my adult years I did indulge in promiscuous behavior. I will admit I was very fast as a teenager and that itself put me in bad situations. When we moved to Chapel Hill, the home of the Tarheels, I was thirteen years old and I lost my virginity two years later around my fifteenth birthday.

Although my mom was completely open with me about sex, I was afraid to tell her when I was ready. It was too early for me to think about sex but most of my friends were already sexually active. I felt ready and in love with my boyfriend. I've heard real horror stories about some of my girlfriends first times having sex. I'm grateful mine wasn't a horrific experience. I can say it was a beautiful time because we were in love. My first love and I are still friends to this day which is crazy to me. We took different paths as we both got married, had children and now in our forties, we are still friends.

In addition to being sexually active, I began to rebel terribly. When I couldn't see my boyfriend or be around him, I would leave the house. There were many nights I snuck him in or I would sneak out. My mom would punish me but that didn't work because I would just leave again. I continued doing it over and over until she got tired and let me be. It was good for a little while until I had to compete with grown women in the neighborhood who didn't have rules or age limitations to the things they could do. He eventually started dealing with this older woman who had a place in our projects. I got tired of it so I moved on and started dealing with a twenty-one-year-old man who was in the Army and had a nice ass Camaro.

In the nineties it was common for older men to deal with teenage girls and not get in trouble. We dealt with these men because they spoiled us and had their own places and cars. Try that mess now and you're definitely going down for statutory rape.

I was fifteen-years old when I began dating and having sex with a guy who was twenty-one years old. I did this after I got mad at my first love for cheating with the older woman. Dating a twenty-one-year-old man was common back then so no he didn't get in trouble. My mom was livid and didn't approve of the relationship at all. My sister told my mom I had a hickey from him and she slapped the living crap out of me. It's not funny but how did I think I was going to get away with messing with him and my mother not find out? Chapel Hill is a small town so news travels fast.

After my mother found out I was sexually active with my first love, as a pre-caution she put me on the Norplant a birth control that lasted five years. I took that as I could have as much sex as I wanted but I was careful because of STDs. I continued with the older guy up until my mother sent me to New York with my nana to finish High School. While I was there this dude drove to New York to see me. We were having sex whenever and however we could even in his car and my nana had no clue. I guess since they knew I was having sex they felt it was no way they could stop me. Eventually it became an 'as long as I don't catch you, your good' situation which was the wrong move because that shit only made me worse. I think I should have had more guidance and discipline. My mom was so wrapped up in her own problems that she just wasn't equipped to deal with me. This is where we should have incorporated family time and trips. Instead the same behaviors from the past was repeated. My mother just didn't have the financial stability to give us what we needed.

I really thought me and this grown man were going to be together forever. I didn't care honey I thought I was grown and just knew we were in love, but I quickly learned I didn't know anything. Messing with him was just a way to piss off my first love because he was damn near screwing the whole damn neighborhood. I wanted to get revenge which I did but I also got my karma because the older dude started messing with girls from the same damn neighborhood too. So, instead of living life as a teenage girl, doing things like going to the mall, high school games and slumber parties I was devastated over a grown man at fifteen years old.

In the fall, I started going to Tilden High School in Brooklyn. I attended this school it while I was with my grandmother back in Brooklyn. I met a guy who I really liked that became my new boo, we'll call him New York.

The Naked Truth

New York was different from what I was used to and had me doing a whole lot of crazy mess. I was meeting him at my friends and cousin's houses to smoke cigarettes and weed. He kept my mind off my ex and North Carolina and I started to enjoy New York's wild side. Maybe a little too much if I must say so myself.

He was so rugged and I got use to the country boys. I can say I enjoyed our little adventurous relationship of basement parties, jumping subway turnstiles and smoking. However, I missed my mother and siblings so I eventually moved back to North Carolina. No sooner than I moved back down south New York got shot and killed in what was said a set up. I was deeply hurt but I think me being in North Carolina helped me get over it a lot faster than I would of if I had been up there. He and my Uncle Ron's deaths tore me down during that time. My uncle was like my dad in a sense. He took me to school and picked me up. He helped me with homework and had me doing chores around the house. I loved him so much and he spoiled me rotten. I can say after them I shut down more and rebelled terribly.

When I got back to Chapel Hill, I was out of control and disobedient to my mother, which I regret every day. My mom would drink most of the day, but she made sure we had hot meals every night. There were times I didn't understand how she did it.

After the school year was over in 1994, my mother decided to move to Raleigh. I didn't want to leave my first love who I eventually got back together with after New York's murder. We did eventually move to Raleigh that next year, but I was able to visit Chapel Hill since I had friends there. I knew my first love was going to mess with other women in the neighborhood, so I resented my mother for making me move. She knew I wasn't happy in Raleigh at first so she would let me go to Chapel Hill to stay weekends with an older friend. My mom trusted her but I learned she wasn't to be trusted at all.

It was one visit to Chapel Hill that changed my life in September 1994. I stayed at my friend's house who my mother trusted to watch me and she had some friends over. Of course, we were drinking everything from forty-ounces of Old English, Gin, and Mad Dog 2020. We were also smoking weed on top of that, my little 105-pound body should not have been consuming all that.

Well, I eventually passed out in her bathroom and all I remember is going to throw up. Next thing I woke up in her bed smelling like throw up and in just a T-shirt. My body felt like I had been run over by a truck but basically that was my first hangover. My stomach was sick and I had a headache, and felt fatigued, but I knew something was not right.

My body didn't feel right and the girl who I was visiting came in the bedroom and was like, "So you are telling me you don't remember nothing?"

I'm confused as to what she is talking about, so I respond something like, "No I just remember throwing up."

Let me say this, I was sixteen-years-old, and she was twenty-two-years-old. My mother trusted her so that is why she let me go to Chapel Hill with her. She began to tell me that two of my classmates and two older men in their mid to late twenties all had sex with me in her bathroom. Mind you, I was out cold and unconscious so I had no idea of what was going on. If I'd been up knowing me, I would have dug them so deep in their eyes. I can't explain how I felt in that moment but I was disgusted and ashamed. I had been gang raped and she did nothing to protect me. What kind of friend was this? Who could think this was funny? After that I didn't trust too many women and I cut her ass off completely.

When it was time for me to go home, I was afraid to let my mom know. I knew she would be so disappointed in me and upset with my so-called friend she trusted me with. When I didn't come home when I was supposed to, my mother and step-dad picked me up. It took me a little while to tell my mother what happened but when I did, I felt a sense of relief. She immediately took me to the clinic along with my baby aunt and got me checked out. There I was at sixteen-years-old diagnosed with chlamydia and gonorrhea, which I had no idea what either of them really was. I just knew I had a sexually transmitted disease and couldn't even say who gave it to me. The nurse gave me some antibiotics, condoms, and counseling about the situation. I heard the so-called friend of mine was going around saying negative stuff about me, but she would meet her own demise later on down the line with her own daughter. See I had to learn as an adult that God takes care of people far better than we can. I was a product of my environment and a lot of things I had done I knew better, no excuses.

The situation haunted me for years but somehow, I pushed it to the back of my mind and kept it moving. It made me forget about Chapel Hill and just focus on finishing school. I just wanted to make my mother proud of me because I felt like I let her down enough already at that time.

I focused on school and getting my high school diploma. I was determined to make my mother and grandparents proud. In the midst of going to school I was starting to enjoy Raleigh, especially our neighborhood at the time, Melvid Court off Peyton Street. I especially saw a change in my family dynamic and household. My mom even started working towards her sobriety at that time. We went from a two bedroom to a three bedroom within a few months. I just really started to enjoy Raleigh and Chapel Hill and the people became a mere memory. My mom and step-dad even got married that October in 1995. His brother came to live with us and yes, we flirted a lot, but at the time I had a boyfriend named Slim. I met Slim at school but he was no good for me. I had a thing for street dudes, drug dealers and that was exactly what Slim was.

One day me and my stepdad's brother were in my mother's living room watching TV and waited until everyone was fast asleep and we had sex. This happened on more than one occasion and I knew it was wrong. I knew if my mother found out she would be highly upset so we kept it a secret. I was that girl who like stepping in the fire no matter how hot it was. The situation didn't last long though because I really did like Slim, but he was a cheater and chicks in Raleigh knew him.

To make me feel secure, he asked his mother to let me move in with them. She said yes only if I kept going to school and I did. I loved his mother, and she loved me. I guess my mom got tired of trying to keep me in the house, so she let it go. As long as I went to school, she didn't push the issue for me to come home.

I dated Slim up until I met my ex-husband at his sister's house on my graduation night. Now her house was the hang out and we had fun. It was where you can meet up, drink, smoke and listen to music, all things I loved to do at eighteen years old. Me and the sister became cool and I eventually moved in with her after the street dude Slim got violent and put his hands on me. He slapped me one time busting my lip and pulled my earrings out my ear splitting my holes open. It only took him one time and my butt got out of there. I thanked his mother for everything, but I saw my mother go through way too many abusive relationships. I always promised myself that I wouldn't do it.

Me and my ex-husband started dating when we were both eighteen years old. The relationship was rocky from the start because he was in the streets too. He was constantly getting locked up and I waited every time. I dealt with a lot of disrespect from his family and it made me a very bitter person. After nine years together we decided to get married which shouldn't have ever happened. We weren't ready and I should have healed from my past first. I mean my second son is named after one of the women he was cheating with which was a coincidence. I was the chick that was spoiled by men in the past and they loved me. I was willing to get freaky in the bedroom so my mate didn't have a reason to cheat. I learned early that doesn't work because when a man wants to stray there's nothing you can do to make them stay.

I was out here giving my jewel to men who weren't worthy because I thought that meant they loved me or I loved them. I later realized that my cookie should not have been shared with a man just because I liked them or was attracted to them. I should have waited until the time was right and I was old enough to understand what came with sex. I didn't give myself or my mind time to grow and know who I was. I felt if I didn't give a man sex, then he wouldn't want me or he would go cheat. Little did I know these jerks will do that anyway weather you give them all the sex they want or not. This behavior eventually followed me on to my adult life. I can truly admit at thirty-seven years old I finally got it. I can say that because I began practicing celibacy and it's helped me gain clarity on men.

    I learned that God has built our bodies to be sacred. Not saying I wouldn't mind getting a tune up every now and then, I'm just not rushing it no more. When you go through so much with men, sex becomes a non-factor. I now know having a faithful man who is committed to me is way more important than just laying with someone you see no future with which I am guilty of. I have dealt with men just to have companionship because I didn't know how to be alone after my marriage. I had a moment and realized I had to think about my children and my health. Once God opened my eyes, I knew that I no longer wanted to sleep with men who I wasn't going to have a future with. Ladies protect your jewel because if we don't nobody else will.

    Luke 16:11 So if you have not been trustworthy in handling worldly wealth, who will trust you with true riches?

    If you can't commit, how can you be faithful?

Chapter 4

Art of Openness
♥ ♥ ♥ Unbreak My Heart ♥ ♥ ♥

    I carried my childhood anger into my relationships as I got older, especially in my marriage. My ex-husband and I met when we were both eighteen-years-old and ended our marriage together, became parents, and got married. I never realized that I wasn't ready for all that until we separated in June 2012. I say that because once I got out of my marriage, I ran the streets like a twenty-one-year-old. I dressed more provocatively, drank a whole lot more, went back to smoking weed, and the worse of all I would leave my children at home just to party. Sounds Familiar? Basically, I fell victim to the life I knew all too well as a child. I didn't realize the separation was void to my sons also. I should have sat down, had faith, and continued to be a mother to them. Instead, I chose what I felt was right at the time which was to self-medicate with alcohol and drugs to numb my pain.

    Their dad is with a woman who was a family friend as well as our neighbor. No, me and her didn't have a relationship, but we knew her and her husband at the time well enough that those boundaries should not have been crossed. That devastated me the most out of all the infidelity I encountered in my marriage. I asked him numerous times why this woman (if we can call her that) wouldn't speak to me. I later learned she didn't speak because she simply wanted my ex-husband. So yes, she did the right thing because had we even talked a little, I would have been on the First 48 serving a life sentence.

    I was so enraged by this betrayal that I let it consume me for three whole years. My whole marriage was filled with lies, cheating, financial issues, arguing, and fighting. All my pregnancies were stressful, miserable and not to mention I lost my one and only daughter in the process. Losing two of the most important things I had, my daughter and my family devastated me for a while. I had been with him for almost 17 years so I didn't really know how to start over. I just knew life as I knew it had changed forever.

Tamika Melvin

After my ex-husband and I separated, my oldest son turned to the blood street gangs. I blame it on my negligence as a mother and his father, who was being more of a friend to him. I should have been there more than ever for the boys at that fragile time in their life. I didn't get him the therapy he needed when he lost his baby sister or when we separated. I never realized how those situations affected him the most being he was my oldest child at thirteen-years old. I was extremely broken and should have sought counseling early on. Instead, I continued to self-medicate my pain with marijuana, alcohol, and partying. Although those things made me feel better for the moment, it wasn't healthy for me or my children. I knew I had to find peace with the situation and what I was doing was not the way.

When you deal with so much disloyalty and strife in your life it can cause you to be a little doubtful about who you are as a person. You can be around people all day every day and still feel self-absorbed. I had always been a person who went for whatever I set my mind to. Around my late twenties and early thirties, I became stagnant and comfortable. Somewhere in between becoming a woman, mother, and a wife I lost myself. I lost who Tamika was trying to please others. Yeah, I was favored by my nana, as my family loves to state, but that doesn't mean I didn't deal with insecurities growing up. I was light skin and still didn't feel pretty no matter how many people told me so.

What people don't understand is just like dark skin girls dealt with people's mean comments so did light skin girls. Yeah, I know your like it's not as common as dark-skinned girls, but it does happen. I had people who treated me mean just because of me being spoiled, light skin with pretty eyes, and because I like to dress nice. People thought just because I was light skin, I didn't go through a hard time. I was called pale, big forehead, no color, cat eyes, things that tore me down mentally, but because I wasn't dark skin it wasn't taken the same way. I'm not saying I didn't get love don't get me wrong, but I did have things I felt insecure about.

The Naked Truth

As we grew up as teens my mother couldn't afford to keep up with things me and my sister needed. We didn't have necessities that was needed like pads, toothpaste, and deodorant. I remember having to use tissue for pads and bleeding through my pants at school in the eighth grade. My mother didn't drive so I had to tie a jacket around my waist and reek of blood all day. I remember feeling so embarrassed, but it was nothing I could do about it. We had days we went to school without deodorant and would be musty by the end of the day.

I remember going to Raleigh one time in particular to visit my aunt and I got some deodorant from her house because we didn't have any. I didn't think she would mind because she had a few different ones. Well, that blew up in my face because she found out and the clothes, she had given me she took back and gave to a neighbor. I was so hurt and embarrassed. Yes, I should have just asked her for it but me being an aunt to my six nieces I definitely would have tried to see the reason they didn't just ask me. I was wrong for stealing it but no one really knew or cared what we were going through. We were living in Chapel Hill and my mom only cared about having her beer as long as she fed us, she felt it was enough but it wasn't.

We also weren't going to the dentist like we should have been even though we had Medicaid. This negligence led to my sister having gum disease and being hospitalized as a child to get her teeth pulled. She then grew up with insecurities as well. I knew my mom was trying her best to raise all four of us on her own, but she just couldn't do it. We lacked necessities which led my sister and I into the wrong things like selling drugs and guys who sold drugs. My mother didn't have the means to take care of us alone. I ended up quitting school in eleventh grade and living off my boyfriend at the time, my first love.

When Mommy and my stepdad became an official couple and moved the family to Raleigh N.C. the summer of 1994 our situation changed. They both had jobs, as a matter of fact my stepdad had two jobs. I went back to school to get my diploma and worked part time, and when my sister turned fifteen years old, she started working at McDonalds. My stepdad made life easier for us once we moved. I will always love him for giving us a better life than we had.

I didn't want to move at first, but after a while I started to love Raleigh. The circumstances around my rape made me face a different form of uncertainty about myself. I was questioning whether I deserved it or not since I was drinking when I wasn't supposed to. I found myself crying and becoming really depressed. I was ashamed of what people thought about me. Even though I did nothing wrong, I blamed myself for that night so many times.

I met Slim while attending Wake Tech Adult High School he was what you would call a bad boy. Bad boys are the ones who sold drugs, drove crack head cars, smoked weed and got janky hotel rooms. In my lost little mind, I thought this was the life when in all actuality I was looking for comfort and love in the wrong damn places. Now that I'm older I see I should have had counseling after the rape situation, but I didn't want to deal with it.

My mother was working at the time and just like I did with everything else I put it in the back of my mind. I dealt with a lot of backlashes from people in Chapel Hill who were saying the woman I stayed with was going around telling people that I knew what went on. I truly did not so that shit was hurtful. She ended up coming to my mother's house back in 2001 and of course I let her have it because why would you lie on me? She apologized but years later as I said she was met with her own demised with her own daughter. People don't believe what goes around comes around and you can't escape karma. After that incident me and her friendship was never the same.

For a while I just didn't trust people like that no more especially women. I'm not saying I'm an angel by no means, but I was never one who tried to do things to hurt my friends intentionally. If I love you, I love you wholeheartedly it was no question about that. The older I got the more I learned that women aren't always going to get along. I've had friends who viewed me as a showoff or bragger which is not me at all. When I became an adult, I worked extra hard to get the things I wanted. I never looked for handouts, I did what I had to do to make things happen. Although I had women in my circle who saw that as boasting or gloating that was never the case. I just have always been a determined person even as a child.

The fact that I had people in my circle for most of my life who viewed me in that kind of light was really scary. These are people that I would do anything for, and to have that type of reality revealed made me become a different person. It made me aggressive and have my guard up a lot more. I was skeptical of new people but I had to be more open to new relationships if I wanted my business to grow. I was done with drama and the hurt that comes with it. If anyone knows me then you know I'm a very open person when it comes to things I've been through. I learned I couldn't confide in everybody because some people are just there to hear the negative things. God gave me the spirit of discernment which helps me to read people for who they really are. You definitely have to know people intentions for you.

❤ ❤ ❤ Love is Blind ❤ ❤ ❤

I had a very dark time in my life when my marriage ended in June 2012 due to infidelity. I felt like I didn't have not one person to lean on. I started to doubt there was a God because what I was going through. I felt like any and everything I loved was taken away from me and I didn't understand why. My confidence went down tremendously. My ex didn't just cheat one time but the whole marriage. It made me feel like I was unattractive and not good enough so I gave up on everything including myself.

I started to hate how I looked physically so I started resenting having children and starved myself. I was drinking, smoking, and not eating properly. I let my insecurities consume me and started dealing with things that I wouldn't normally have dealt with. Most of the men I dated afterwards were losers and really couldn't give me what I felt I deserved. I was dating all these young dudes trying to get some of my youth back and feel wanted. However, that didn't work it just made my insecurities worse. I was used to a man taking care of home but instead I was running into these men who didn't get the concept of a man's position in the household.

I can admit that I let men treat me like an option and not a priority. I think I was feeling like maybe that's what I deserved and there were no good men out here anymore. Social media was at full bloom at this point and men became more disrespectful and less romantic to women. There was no longer communication or men who wanted to wine and dine women anymore.

I dealt with things from men I wouldn't have ever dealt with in the past. I was completely off the dating scene for seventeen years and these men in 2012 had become extremely needy. I dated dudes that were living off me, driving my car, selling drugs, couldn't keep a job, just came home from prison, mama's boys, insecure, emotional, broken, and abusive. Yeah, I knew better but I was hurt and looking for love in all the wrong places. I engaged with men who weren't good for me or my children. Why did I continue to deal with these types of men? All I can say is I had to really be desperate to look over all the red flags.

At some point I got comfortable and that did nothing but bring me trouble. I eventually got fed up with men and decided to cut off sex and relationships for a while. I began to practice celibacy because I needed some clarity in my life. Most dating didn't last no longer than four months. I should have been working on loving myself and getting a divorce. I'm going to give you all a little back story on my dating life.

There was a dude, I will call him Country, I met him at a strip club name The Pitt back in 2013 but I never really loved him. I used him for comfort, money, and sex. I used him for five years because I knew I could. I talked to him like he was nothing and I didn't care.

Well karma came to my door in January 2018, literally. Country came by my house like he was bringing me something for my car. I asked him to leave because I didn't feel like being bothered that day, he was a big liar and always in a financial bind. Little did I know he was fed up with my bullshit. Without any warning this punk punched me in my face, ran, jumped in his car and drove off.

I went through months of stalking, harassment, restraining orders, court and gun purchases. I was angry but after thinking about how I treated him, even though it's never okay for a man to hit a woman, I understood his frustration. I eventually forgave him but I never tried to do that again, it wasn't right. I was taking out the anger from my marriage on men who had nothing to do with it.

I dated another guy that we'll call V.A. He treated me like a queen but I had my guard up, or so I thought. He was a complete gentleman from the beginning and for a few months we were inseparable. I mean he cooked, cleaned, bonded with my boys, and just had a very laid-back aura about himself. I thought this was it for me and I found my Mr. Right. He made me forget about all I had gone through in my past.

I dated him in 2015 during a time I was on break from Country. I later found out V.A. was on the run and didn't tell me anything about it. I was pissed, hurt and devastated because he was the first man since my separation from my marriage that made me feel good about myself. The US Marshals came to my home while my youngest son was there with him and I was at work. He had used my address to look for a daytime job because he cleaned buildings at night and they tracked him there. Not to mention, I was pregnant and had just gotten an abortion a month and a half prior to this shit. I just couldn't believe he didn't tell me he was on the run or even facing gun charges. The first man I really connected with in every way was now gone. I felt like I couldn't win for losing and became angry with myself for giving him a chance.

Yeah, I know what y'all saying, another convict? I thought he was a stand-up guy after I witnessed him with his daughter while she was down for the summer. He was very attentive and nurturing to her. However, he lied to me about the whole gun altercation, his relationship with his daughters' mother, and his prison sentence. I was livid but I forgave him. I loved him but at the end of the day he understood that I needed peace in my life. I eventually moved on because I knew I deserved a better hand than what I was dealt. So, I eventually let it go and moved on. Men continued to show me who they were and I eventually moved on accordingly.

After dealing with sorry dudes, I decided to take a break from men entirely. My focus became me and my three boys because at that point I had no time to waste. I was getting older and before I turned forty, I needed to build something that my boys could carry on. Building a solid foundation was my main focus. No more being insecure about my age and scared to put myself out there to network. I didn't mind having male friends, but no strings attached and no friends with benefits. At my age, I wasn't interested in getting into anything else that was inconsistent. My decision to be celibate gave me so much clarity on what I really wanted in a relationship. I had started to question if God was punishing me for not working on my marriage. I loved my ex-husband but if I stayed the cheating would have continued. God knows it didn't help that my own people ran around with him. That relationship along with others tore down my self-esteem and trust for years. So when I lost my nana and mommy, the only people I felt who loved and understood me unconditionally, I made a terrible decision and got into a horrible relationship.

I was basically three years into my celibacy but broke it when I met this nothing ass dude June 2019. No man is worth your diamond until they prove themselves worthy, so why I kept making the same mistake is beyond me. During one of the most vulnerable times of my life I began to date this guy whom we shall call Malice. I thought Malice was my knight and shining armor. I mean I was ready to have another baby, get married and buy a home with this man. He was the true meaning of a wolf in sheep's clothing and everything that glitters ain't gold.

I lost my nana on March 2nd, 2019, and my mother had just been placed under hospice at the time we met. He came at a time I was dealing with depression, grief, bitterness and regret. I tried to go on like everything was okay but I was dying inside. I hadn't seen my nana since August 29th, 2018, because my family was at odds at that time but that will be later discussed. My mom only lived a month after I got in this relationship. When my mom left me and I no longer had my grandmother to lean on I leaned on him and my friends.

    I have always had a strained relationship with the family so I wanted to feel loved. Malice had red flags from the beginning of the relationship, so why didn't I just leave him alone? I should have had faith and took that time to mourn my nana and prepare for the loss of my mother. I let loneliness get the best of me and dealt with a narcissist. Once I saw the first sign of inconsistency the relationship should have been over. We moved entirely too fast and I was homeless living with my best friend when we met. Hell, I stayed homeless until I left him alone completely but we will get into that in a minute.

    I didn't know this man and jumped in the relationship headfirst. I didn't follow my gut instinct because I was worried about other people talking and their opinions. Honey I will be the first to say THAT WAS MY BIGGEST MISTAKE!

    Everything started off okay. We were planning on saving and getting a place of our own. However, he was spending the money just as quick as we saved it. On several occasions while I was preoccupied with my family or late at night he would leave and spend $100 to $200 dollars at a time. He blamed it on gambling but I knew something just wasn't right.

    Malice jumped from job to job and didn't keep one long at all, which frustrated me. I wasn't just struggling alone, now I had a bum ass dude leaning on me too. Now my mom and nana were gone and I couldn't bare being alone at that time. We were staying with my best friend and then moved in with my aunt that November 2019. I really didn't know this man like that but my best friend and aunt accepted him on the behalf of me. I knew I had to get out the relationship when he became insecure, emotional and abusive. He was jealous of any man that came around and my other female best friend who is gay. It was really beginning to irritate me that I had to explain who people were that I've known for years. I can't stand an insecure man so I knew the relationship would come to an end.

The move with my aunt started to become a bad idea. It was so much coming to me from outsiders and at that point I was tired of the family drama nonsense. Malice became very aggressive and mean, but I didn't know how to get rid of him. He was a con artist and a big liar but I loved him, or so I thought. On Christmas eve we got into a big argument at the house while my aunt was out for the night. It got so bad that it almost got physical and I had to grab a knife. He apologized and my crazy ass let him back in without saying anything to my family.

We got through Christmas and then my niece had a birthday party in my uncle's apartment complex. Someone told me that one of my close friends looked like she had an accident on Capital Boulevard so we raced to see if she was okay. Malice got upset because I said he was driving reckless as we went down Fox Road behind Target and Old Navy. This dude got so mad that he spun the car around almost in a donut and drove through a wooded area screaming, "We can both die!"

I yelled to the top of my lungs as I begged him to please stop and when he did, I punched him in the face and ran and Target. I went to the bathroom and realized I left my whole purse in the truck including my cell phone. I calmed myself down because I had to go back to my uncle's house. I didn't want them to see me upset or know what's going on but I knew I had to get away, but how? I got back in the car and we rode back in silence like nothing ever happened. If anybody knows me, I definitely was in a dark place because my temper usually is on ten. I let a sorry man con me and get in my head to think he really didn't mean what he was doing.

New Year's Eve we went to church with his mom and brought it in. For a few days things were okay but on January 6th, 2020, everything came to a head. I was almost dead broke and had to ask my son for $40 so I can get gas to get to and from work. I was sleeping that morning and at five a.m. I heard my grandfather who lived with us go open the door. He knocked on the door to let me know that Malice knocked on his window and woke him up to open the door.

I was livid, who does that to an eighty-six-year-old man? I went in the bedroom next door where he tried to go to sleep and saw he looked high off something. I slapped the hell out of him and ran to tell my aunt what happened. She said he had to go but he raced out the house, jumped in the truck and drove off. He had stolen all my money out my purse and left me with nothing. I was so hurt and embarrassed but I now knew that he wasn't gambling this bastard with an addict.

I went to work and carried on my day but my name was on the truck so I had to get it back before he did something to it or wrecked it. I called the police. They located the truck and my sister's fiancée, and I went to pick it up. I knew then we were done. Of course, he kept calling, begging, and threatening me so I had to come up with a plan. He couldn't know where I was at and I didn't want to bring that drama to my aunt's house.

I needed to get back on a spiritual realm, so I hooked up with some ladies at an art gallery who I still have contact with today. We talked, cried, shared, and most of all prayed together. They helped me come up with a strategy to move out the house and get rid of him for good. I didn't feel comfortable there anymore and didn't want to involve my family. I came up with a plan and moved out the house waiting for tax time to come so I can get a place of my own.

That didn't sit well with my aunt so of course she got upset and got my cousins involved and they were mad at me too. At that point I really didn't care, I had to do what I felt was best and safe for my people at the time. My son took the truck as his own and I moved back with my best friend.

About a month had passed and he told me he had gotten some help and apologized. I believed him like a crazy person but I told him he had to prove himself. He came into town for Valentine's weekend and we agreed to go out for dinner but nothing more. I told my best friends I was spending Valentine's with them and I should have. The night before we were at my best friend house with two of my stud friends drinking and enjoying ourselves. He got his mom's car and came to pick me up so I wouldn't drink or drive. I let the alcohol alter my judgement and went with him to his mother's house.

    I went to the bathroom to take a shower and when I came out the whole house was pitch black. This bastard picked me up off my feet by my neck, rushed me in the room, and threw me on the bed, closing the room door. It was dark so I couldn't see anything, but I was fighting with all I had in me.

    He then pinned my arms down with his knees, putting all his weight on my chest and choked me with both hands until I almost lost my breath. I saw my life flash before my eyes. I saw my mother, my nana crying, and my kids crying, it was dark but his eyes were of the devil. I didn't know this man at all. All I could do was cry and pray because I didn't think I was going to make it.

    I felt my life slipping and his mother must have heard us and busted in the room smacking him. I jumped up gasping for air and throwing whatever was in reach until I was able to run outside. It was cold, dark and I was naked so I didn't make it far. I stayed that night and the next day I tried to leave but he just followed me every day after that.

    He threatened to have my son arrested, scare my grandad, harass my aunt, get my best friend put out, get me fired, mess with people's cars I loved just a bunch of crazy mess. I dealt with a restraining order before so let's just say the system failed a lot of these women who have died by the hand of their partners. I definitely wasn't going to be a statistic.

    I eventually told my best friend that I didn't want to be with him anymore but never said why. Either he was gonna die or I was going to prison but I wasn't going to tolerate any more abuse. I watched my mom go through it and promised myself never to do it. I needed to get rid of this man for good and get my life back in order.

The Naked Truth

The incident happened February 13th, 2020, and from that day he wouldn't leave my side. I even had a panic attack at work February 20th and was rushed to the hospital from work. I had plenty of chances to tell people what he had done from Christmas Eve until February 13th but I chose to deal with it on my own. February 26th taxes dropped and I knew he was itching to get high. I prepared myself to say goodbye forever that day and I did. He blew his whole tax return within two days and I was able cut him off completely. I made sure he wasn't able to contact me and I let my job know what was going on.

God gave me a chance for a clean slate and this time I took it. Did I miss him? Yes, but only for the companionship because everything else was a disaster. He was an abusive crackhead narcissist who stole from the woman he supposedly loved so much. I thank the highest for getting me out that situation alive because it could have turned out so much worse.

Love is blind and it took over my mind. I definitely was in a dark place and lost all self-worth to deal with a man of that caliber. My 9mm Ruger got missing but after finding out he was a crackhead I see where it probably went to. I get disgusted with myself every time I think about what I put myself through for a sorry man but everything happens for a reason. I hope someone could relate to this story and it helped them if they were or still are dealing with domestic violence.

When someone is addicted to drugs, they will do whatever they have to do to get their fix. If they are unable to do so you become the target. See the flesh is weak and when you are an addict like he was, you do what you can so you can feel that high. It's sad that he never got real help because if he does, he could be an amazing man for someone. I forgive him and myself for each time I went back but I will never forget February 13th. I am living carefree and unapologetic these days because the last couple of years I took a lot of losses.

Maya Angelou had a saying, "When people show you who they are, believe them the first time." I knew what I was dealing with and insisted on going back more than once. I had to learn to love everything about me without a man. My discernment showed me he was no good early on but I went against what God showed me. He let me sit in it but saved me in the end. Father I thank you for your forgiveness, love, and coverage during that trial. I'm forever grateful.

Chapter 5

Art of Forgiveness
♥ ♥ ♥ Coming to Terms with Reality ♥ ♥ ♥

There's peace in accepting the promise of restoration. So, in order to live my full life, I had to confront the things I was most afraid of. I had to move on from being stagnant by accepting what was and is in my life. I really needed to work through my issues because they were wearing me down.

I had to learn not to give my past so much energy because it was keeping me from building my future. I tried talking to family and friends, going to church, reading self-help books, and even prayer but nothing seemed to work in my favor.

Around springtime in 2020, one of my best friends suggested that maybe I needed to consider talking to a professional. I will be the first to say I wasn't thrilled about going to therapy. I always felt that it wasn't for me to be honest, but the more I read up on major depression the more I knew I needed to get healed mentally.

In April 2018, a month before my fortieth birthday, I started therapy, but I wasn't consistent like I needed to be. After speaking with my primary care doctor in April 2020, who referred me to four therapists, I was ready to get healed.

I was reluctant to follow through but the third therapist I spoke to on the phone made me feel very at ease. I was very open about what I wanted and needed. She assured me she could assist me and we made an appointment for that next week.

Although I was very excited about my journey to healing, it didn't come easy. I had to really unlearn my whole way of thinking at this point. If I wanted to let go of my past, I had to release the guilt and forgive myself and others. I will admit that keeping things bottled up made me bitter, depressed, vulnerable and cruel at times.

Tamika Melvin

When I started my sessions, I had to really get my mind focused. There were things I had to rid myself of and there was no denying that. At that

The Naked Truth

time, I was single, so my mind was clear of men. I had previously been in an abusive relationship with a drug addict and was ready to become celibate again. I was practicing celibacy for four years from 2015 to 2019 but I let the spirit of fear get the best of me. I broke my celibacy for like four months in 2017 but quickly got back on the band wagon. I needed a complete break from men entirely back then. I went on a serious MANCATION, which was much needed.

Although I was drained mentally and scarred emotionally, I continued to give my past energy. When you give your past energy, you rob yourself of things that could possibly make you happy. I started getting in my own way by letting fear control my decisions. I became so afraid of failure that I would give up on events and activities that could have helped me elevate more in my publishing business. By the end of my first set of therapy sessions I was diagnosed with Major Depression disorder.

The first thing we tackled in therapy was letting go of resentment, abuse and guilt. Those were the biggest burdens that I held in my heart. I dealt with a lot of internal traumas and I thought if I didn't speak about it then somehow it would go away. Of course, that's not the case because I became angrier about my childhood. Even though I never spoke to my mom about it in the past I did end up telling her how I felt back in 2018.

The time had come for me to release and renew my mind. I know my mom did all she could to make sure me and my four siblings were good. I watched my mom struggle a lot. I watched her go through a lot of hurt and abuse with men. I too was following the same pattern so before I turned forty-two years old, I made it a point to break this generational transfer. I had to forgive two of my brothers' fathers because if I didn't, I would continue carrying that burden.

All that anger I carried from a child to adulthood turned my heart cold. Once I started acknowledging it, I was able to redirect it and properly neutralize my mind.

Tamika Melvin

I was like a ticking time bomb in the past waiting to explode. When I did explode it wasn't pretty nor am I proud how I handled certain situations. When I went through traumatic situations, I took my anger out on my mom a lot. Not because it was her fault but because I felt like she could have protected me or stood up for me more. For instance, with my oldest brother's father, why didn't she just leave him? When he picked up that chair at me, why wasn't that enough for her to leave?

I know she was just a young woman in love but that didn't mean she didn't love me. I know that now but for years I really didn't think she did. When I heard the things my mom went through growing up, I completely understood why she put up with so much and why she loved so hard. Even when those sorry bastards didn't deserve her heart, she still loved.

The stages of blame I was dealing with were really emotional because I finally got out how I felt about my marriage ending and my daughter's passing. I was angry with my ex and his sister for years but buried it deep so I could co-exist. I did that with many relationships in my life. For years I buried my feelings and tried to continue on with life but internally it was killing me. I was filled with so many emotions most of all anger. The only way to rid myself of that hurt was to let it out and accept what was.

My daughter Shaquoia passed away July 23rd, 2006, from suffocation and overlay. I really didn't know how to address the issue because the overlay was caused by her aunt (her dad's sister). I always wanted to talk to her about it but never knew where to start. I finally decided to talk to her sometime in 2019 before my interview with Iyanla Vanzant and it was weight lifted off my chest. We had never had the conversation amongst ourselves and it was very much needed. I know it wasn't done intentionally but it still didn't change the fact that I was hurting. I felt like when she passed, I was forced to overlook it and move on because it was my ex-husband's sister.

I realize now that our marriage was never the same after our daughter passed. I also blamed my mom because I felt if we didn't argue that night I would have just stayed there. She told me to get out so I went to my ex-husband's sister's house.

My ex-husband sister was sleep on the couch but eventually went to get in her bed in the wee hours of the morning. I was exhausted and fell asleep in his niece's room myself, which was down the hall from his sister room. At the time I was attending church regularly with one of their cousins. His sister didn't know he put the baby in her bed that morning. She was highly intoxicated so she laid on her and that was it, my baby was gone. I found my daughter the next morning unresponsive and dead.

All because I was in a situation that I should not have been in, which was being homeless. I feel like she would have still been here if I was in the proper living situation as I was told by Iyanla Vanzant in a Fix My Life interview in October 2019. She was right because most of my marriage I carried most of the household. I forgive them and myself because it was negligence on all parts but no one can ever tell me how to feel about that situation.

I was also upset with my oldest uncle because the first and only time he saw my daughter was when she was a couple of months old at his house. I remember he cursed out her dad for bringing her in the living room to get her baby bag. It started a big argument and we left his house. I didn't see him anymore until the day she died. Then my baby aunt and I weren't speaking at the time because of a mess I felt she caused between me and my in-laws, so again I hadn't seen or spoken to her in like three months until the day my daughter passed. I had mixed emotions because it's like now everyone is here but to tell you the truth, I didn't really want to deal with none of them or my ex-husband's family at that time. The more I hid my emotions the more enraged I became.

Therapy helped me learn to release the guilt and accept her death. She was my one and only baby girl who I always wanted and like that she was gone at seven months old. I would be lying if I say I don't miss her or cry when I think about what she could have been. I just knew it was time for me to reach a point of acceptance and in time I have. In life people can get over a situation quicker than you and move on quicker than you. It's up to you to take your power back and move on from it.

My divorce was something else I had to come to accept. I got to a place of peace, but it was definitely a long road. See my ex didn't just cheat but it was with someone I kind of expected. Her energy towards me was always so negative but I really didn't think much of it. Her husband and my husband were cool, but my gut always told me she wanted my man, but I didn't have proof. When I left my marriage, it was because I was tired of the infidelity and just not happy.

The week before I left, I had just had a big book signing at Club Taboo's and he didn't show which caused me total embarrassment because my family was there and a few members of his were in attendance, too. Of course, I got questions from guests asking, "Where is your husband?" I was so disappointed, but I held my composure.

After that I decided I had to find an exit plan. Long story short June 7th, 2012, I packed up my four-bedroom house, put my things in storage, and moved in with my mom. Yes, I was scared to start over, but I definitely felt our marriage was over two years prior. During that time back in October 2010 I was told by my doctor I had Trichomoniasis a STD and I knew I wasn't cheating. So why is a married woman is even dealing with a situation like this? I was embarrassed and devastated. We separated for a about a month but for the sake of our marriage, children, and him begging I let him back in which was a big mistake. This dude turned his back and basically said F me two years later. I felt like the biggest dummy on Earth but I tried my best to keep my composure.

I had become so weak and lost myself in so many ways that at the end I had to choose me. Let me say this if people can walk away from you let them walk. Don't force yourself to continue to deal with deceit and betrayal because in the end you will hate that person.

The Naked Truth

I hated my ex for how he handled the situation. If he didn't want me, he could have easily let me know. I had asked on many occasions did he want to work on the marriage. We were married seven years and the whole marriage was filled with infidelity. Don't get me wrong, I had deep rooted anger issues, but the cheating didn't help at all. After three years of being mad in 2015 I finally told him I forgive him, and I want us to have a healthy relationship for the kids. Of course, from then to now we have had our ups and downs, but I can say I am not angry anymore. I'm at peace with that situation and I have God to thank for that.

As for my family, I know it's been unresolved issues with me, my sister, aunt and cousins but a lot of that stemmed from our upbringing. Yeah, I was bad as a child, but I saw and heard so much chaos growing up. Nobody really understood what I fought inside. I had insecurities too but if my family really had time to know and understand that then things could have turned out different.

The family was pulled apart, which wasn't cool because all it did was make us divide and lose two of the most important people of our family tree, Nana and Mommy. I love my family dearly but not enough to disturb my peace but I stand to say I am willing to put in the work to keep us together like Mommy and Nana would want us to be. When loved ones betray you it's hurtful because these are the people you look to for love, but instead you find envy and strife. I accept the fact that we can't change the past, but we are in control of how we proceed in the future as a family.

I have accepted the fact that I dealt with a variety of abusive behaviors growing up, being raped at sixteen, losing my daughter, my relationships failing including my marriage, the downfalls, the betrayals, the guilt of not being a good mother, and most of all I accepted that I was not always a nice person. My advice to you all is never talk anyone into loving, caring, calling, or coming to see you. If you're a factor in their life they will make time. Acceptance is the promise of restoring your life.

God gave my family a wake-up call with my Nana passing in March 2019 and five months later my mother in July 2019. It's up to us to make sure we remain humble and close. How we carry ourselves from here on out will determine the relationship we are trying so hard to keep together. May God continue to cover our family.

1Peter: 3:9 Do not repay evil with evil or insult with insult. On the contrary, repay evil with blessing, because to this you were called so that you may inherit a blessing.

Chapter 6

Process of Elimination
♥ ♥ ♥ Relax, Relate, Release ♥ ♥ ♥

People who I thought were my friends were frauds. I learned everyone who say they love you really don't, they love the things you can do for them. My insecurity and bitterness came because I didn't trust people anymore.

In my opinion I didn't have the moral support I needed from my family, which was not entirely their fault. I wasn't open with them because of things I've heard from others who weren't family. I didn't have real friends who helped me get through things like my daughter's death and my marriage break up.

Dealing with the death of my child, divorce and three kids alone really took a toll on me. I was in a very dark space. I now understand why I was jumping from man to man looking for comfort. I was dealing with toxic relationships in my life just to have a man around. See what I should have been doing was trying to heal myself, love myself, find myself and get Tamika together. I rushed into situations with some sorry men I knew I had no business dealing with. I can't blame anyone but myself because I didn't have faith to stand alone.

I was all about making myself feel good instead of being home mothering my sons. I now know my past had a lot to do with how I handled things with my marriage, friendships, parenting, and life in general. I am thankful for therapy because it challenged me to release so many things, I had bottled up inside me.

Therapy helped me discover that some of my failed relationships were because I was afraid to be transparent and open. I learned that being insecure is not just about looks, but it's also about the uncertainty of life's path God has planned for us. Again, I didn't have faith and thought being hard and not showing emotion was a good thing. Instead, it made things in my life worse and I continued to suppress my feelings even more.

The Naked Truth

One thing I can say I do now is what makes me happy not what makes others happy. I'm doing what I want when I want and I'm not apologetic for it. I use to crave validation and absorb people's opinions until one day I just didn't anymore. The year 2020 became my year of vision and 2021 was my year of manifestation. If God's willing, 2022 will be my year of execution. I promised myself March 10th, 2020, I will go harder than ever for myself and my children. I declared on that day that I will not let anything nor anyone take me back to that dark place.

If anyone brings any negative energy my way, I will carry the whole relationship different. I found a way to distance myself from individuals without being mean about it. Protect your energy by all means, it can eliminate stress, drama and save your life. I use to have excruciating migraines often but after prioritizing my life they have become almost nonexistent. I also learned people aren't going to have the same morals and mindset that you have. Throughout my life I had to build myself up in this corrupt world. I was looking for love in all the wrong people, who had red flags that should have been straight deal breakers.

People always told me, "Meka you have it going on, Meka you're smart, Meka you're beautiful," but if you have low self-esteem, it really doesn't matter what anyone says. All we know is how we're feeling at that time. There were rumors that some of my family members enjoyed and even talked about the fact that I was down and out, had to move a lot, relationships weren't lasting, my oldest son was getting locked up over and over, or I wasn't a good mother. I admit it was all true but that just made me even more prideful with asking for help.

There were a few times me and my children slept in my car after arguing with my mother, I went without eating, went without lights, went without water, and it all just made me stronger. I'm very grateful to God for turn of my circumstances. We're supposed to be living life, not just existing. I had to revamp and regroup things in my life. I had to let some people go and I gained some new people in my life. I can finally say that

I'm on a new high about life. Even though I'm still a work in progress, I am more than how people perceive me.

I know people who are reading this probably will never understand how I kept so much under wraps, but it was because I mastered suffering alone. I learned to do that from the age of six years old and I decided to end it when I turned forty-two years old. I will continue to encourage others to speak up and get help. Fear is one of the reasons we have so many people dealing with mental illnesses. People are afraid to seek the help they need because of others' opinions of them.

I want to be able to show people, it's okay to tackle their issues and not let the issues attack them. They can let go of the skeletons in their closets and heal themselves in the process. I was suffering from a mixture of manic and major depression all because I didn't deal with things from my past. You never realize how much better life could be once you rid yourself of unnecessary baggage.

❤ ❤ ❤ Eliminate to Elevate ❤ ❤ ❤

I contracted the coronavirus in June 2020. I can say that was a true eye opener to me. I literally felt like I was near death while fighting that virus. There were nights I was scared to go to sleep because I was afraid, I wouldn't get back up. I had a fever for thirteen days, sinus pressure, congestion, diarrhea, fatigue, loss of appetite and body aches. The virus lasted from June 16th until July 2nd, 2020. I couldn't stand on my feet, eat any food or even take a shower properly at that time.

I felt like each day I made it through was a blessing because many people died from that very same virus. I think about how grateful we should be for life because dealing with such a sickness I know God had to be with me. During that time as I laid helpless in my bed, I reflected on all the obstacles I had overcame within that year. I prayed and made a promise to God that if I made it through that I would make some changes in my life.

The Naked Truth

I knew the first thing that needed to take place was me getting back the structure in my life. I found myself in a violent life-threatening situation four months prior by the hands of my ex. I definitely needed to learn to love myself and heal instead of just moving past things. When your mental health is not stable it wears down on you.

Losing my grandmother after not seeing her for six whole months before she passed due to drama and nonsense broke me in a major way. I felt so much guilt and pain after that loss because she was my second mother. I regretted the decision, but God knows why I did it. Who wants to continue to deal with people who does spiteful things like befriend your ex and his new girlfriend who broke up your home, invite your ex to family functions, let your ex live with them, befriend your ex and his woman on social media, speak negative things to people before they get to know you, your own family supposedly friends telling you nonsense they say, and the list continues.

I learned to live with it and deal with some family differently. I was angry about a decision that one my cousins made in his marriage making it my own hurt. Why? Because this same cousin would run the streets with my ex-husband while he did his dirt. So yes, I was against the infidelity entirely. I felt like my nana as the matriarch of the family should have been against it too. We were taught to stick by our loved ones no matter right, wrong, or indifferent. I will admit I saw my family use some double standards over my life span but I myself never thought cheating was okay for anybody. I wish I would have let my cousin figure out his own life and stayed out of it. The vengeful and selfish part of me wouldn't let me budge and for that I'm very sorry. Sorry can't bring my grandmother back but we can push forward and do things differently.

After bickering for months, posting things on social media, not speaking to each other and putting outsiders in the mix we all had to come together. Nana was on life support, and I can remember that day like it was yesterday because it was the most surreal moment for us all. It was just like that we came together like nothing happened. I replay the situation over in my head but I had to move past it because God knows why I distanced myself. I didn't stay away to be malicious, but I was tired of the drama that was going on within my family.

No, I'm not perfect but I didn't want to deal with that drama anymore. I've encountered that with my family all my life and at some point, I had to rid myself of it. We must understand that we can't rid ourselves of lifetime relationships, which is our family. However, we can choose how and when to deal with them. After losing Nana and Mommy I promised myself that I will keep my distance from the drama but without provoking anger. My family now knows if I feel like something is beginning to be too much I will nicely pull away. I never want to lose another family member in the middle of chaos like we lost my grandmother.

Covid taught me to cherish the family time I do have but also to build a sturdy foundation for my own children, especially when I learned I was having a grandchild. I decided to finish my degree and I had five months to do it with twenty-two credits left. I got focused on God and He blessed me tremendously from July 2020 until now I have elevated to a level I can't even explain. I will say I know I couldn't have done it without the highest, our father in heaven.

After covid I also had to rid myself of seasonal relationships I had with gutter people who did gutter things. See no matter how long I've known people I had to let go and love them from a distance. I have dealt with many opportunists which had to stop. You don't realize these things until certain circumstances occur in your life.

You can't trust people who are not emotionally healthy because they will hurt you because they're hurting. Have you ever heard the saying, "Hurt people, hurt people?" Well, that is a true statement and I can say I've been on both sides of the track. I have hurt people because I was unhappy and going through. I wanted you to be just as miserable as me. I would say things I know would hurt others just because I wasn't happy with my life.

The Naked Truth

I learned from therapy and my current relationship that I had to eliminate negative conversations and drama around me. I wanted to be great, so I had to deal with people who provoked greatness. I started talking in the direction I wanted my life to go.

No, the road wasn't easy because when God gives you power you have to get ready for pain. We have to understand sometimes in order to win the fight we can't always go in the ring. I pray and meditate now more than I ever have before. I had to purge myself from smoking, drinking and partying so much. I needed a complete cleanse and after meeting the love of my life he helped me do just that. Gods sometimes sees our suffering and brings us relief. Malice had to go and God saw fit to help me rid myself of that toxic relationship. I know now I can love again, have joy again, be vulnerable again, and most of all have a loyal husband.

The year 2020 has been one of the most successful years of my life. I acquired getting a screenwriting job, wrote four books, obtained my B.A. in English and Creative Writing with a minor in Screenwriting, started a nightwear line, got engaged, rode a plane or the first time, became a certified life coach, quit smoking and started the process to have my house built all in one year. I can say I'm really living my best life and am no longer just existing. I never wanted to embrace change but I'm glad I have because nothing, but elevation came once I did.

Chapter 7

Path of Spirituality not Religion
♥ ♥ ♥ God in Me ♥ ♥ ♥

I will be the first to say that I grew up and up until recent years didn't fully believe in God. Growing up in Brooklyn I never had the religious background as I saw practiced so much in North Carolina. Therefore, I never really knew about faith, patience or prayer.

I mean yes, my mother and Nana taught me the basic like saying my grace and prayers before bed but it was never consistent. I remember seeing a few friends go to catholic school, some were Jehovah witness, and some were Muslims but I never really understood religion at all. My nana took me to church quite a few times but because it wasn't a regular thing, I would get bored and be ready to leave.

I moved to Raleigh North Carolina in 1990 after fighting and getting jumped at Junior High School in New York. I wasn't scared but my mother was. When I got down south, I will say my baby aunt was the first person who introduced me to what having a church home was really like. We were going to church and bible study every week. Me and my cousin even had to have a bible verse a week. I can say that taught me my first lessons of what church people are really like LOL. I still thank her for the experience but let's just say that's why I don't attend churches now.

I don't knock those that do but I definitely pray and stay in my word at home. I have attended many churches, but I joined four throughout my years here on this earth. Let me just say the experiences were not so good. I wasn't understanding why I couldn't grab hold to the word but then one day God gave me clarity.

After my mother passed, I kept having this reoccurring dream about her screaming and crying. I was homeless at the time living with my aunt. I would pray every morning and night for God to give me a sign. I didn't know if she didn't want me in the house, she passed away in. I continued having that dream until I left Malice completely alone. When I cut all contact that is when the blessings came pouring in. I robbed myself of peace way too long and it was time to take my power back.

Once I was fully over Covid I enrolled back in therapy and hired a life coach because I needed to get back to my true self. It wasn't just for me but for my children also. Fervently I prayed every day and night looking to God for guidance. The calling I had on my life was bigger than me but first I had to learn to be obedient. Being alone really makes you understand who God is because he reveals himself most when you're alone. I had to push myself to have faith even when I didn't have the answers. It was a point in time that if I didn't have any type of companionship or friends around, I would get lonely and depressed.

It was days I thought about suicide and cried to God for guidance. I had no faith and was a very negative person. I'm grateful for the spiritual people I've encountered these last couple of years. God knows it's been days I wanted to end it all, but I thought about how it would affect my children. My boys need me because when it comes down to it, I'm all they really have.

That was the trick of the enemy. We should never become so mentally unstable that we anticipate to take our own life. It's ungodly and selfish to think that way especially when you know better. There are people who are really sick mentally and have no one to help or guide them. I prayed those demons off and asked for forgiveness because nothing and no one should ever make you think that selfishly. I knew I had to continue praying for God to heal my heart and mind. Mental stability was what I needed and I worked hard to get it.

The Bible says to walk by faith and not by sight because you can't see when you're in a storm. God doesn't feed on insecurities so you have to have a goal for your life. Never be comfortable with less than what God has planned for your life. Our circumstances are just that, they are not who we are as a person. With that being said, I accepted God as my author and finisher of life. I had to create new order in my life and if wanted new blessings. We all know we can't get new blessings with the old order of living.

❤ ❤ ❤ Are You Ready ❤ ❤ ❤

In our lifetime we ask God for many things, but the question is are we ready for it? We must be prepared for what we are praying for because if not we can ruin it. When you are ready for change you must execute a plan and act on it. I found the blessing in the lessons I've encountered in my life. The mistakes that I have made were because I didn't fully prepare myself for what I asked God for.

I wanted to be an entrepreneur but was I organized enough to do it? I wanted a husband but was I living like a wife? I wanted a family but was I able to support them? I wanted to move on to live my best life but was I healed? The answer was no because I still had work to do. I didn't understand why nothing was working out for me. God saves us from ourselves sometimes that we don't even realize it at that moment. God can open doors for us and we can close them just by speaking negative. I had to train myself to speak positivity over my life. If I thought I couldn't write books or people wouldn't like my writing I wouldn't have written four books this year. I had to trust in my father's guidance so I can continue to be righteous in my walk.

I have heard so many people throughout my walk of life say they want things to happen but never are they ready for the change. You have to be ready to give up the things you love most to get the very thing that's good for you. I couldn't pursue being a life coach, successful author and screenwriter while smoking cigarettes, overindulging in alcohol and partying all the time. I was high all the time and drinking to numb the pain of losing my mother and grandmother. I was living day to day self-medicating as I tried to bury my guilt and grief. I had to quit or at least eliminate those things if I wanted to move past that stage in my life. I knew those were some of the things that we're hindering me from being my best self.

Tamika Melvin

I knew once I implemented change in my life, I would lose people. I wasn't the same Meka no more so people felt I was acting funny or being controlled by my fiancée. Nope not the case at all it was me wanting more for my life. I wasn't doing the same things as my family and friends no more so I was talked about. The old me use to care about other people's opinions of me but the changes I made were a true blessing to my life.

This is what I meant about being ready for the change. We have to set those boundaries and limitations with the relationships we chose to encounter in our lives to elevate to the next level. If we don't, we will find ourselves being people pleasers and not being pleasing to God or ourselves.

My destiny is not tied to what others think of me anymore but what God says I am. He doesn't bless us by other opinions of us so why should we care. We have to have faith to stand alone because if not we're always going to be dependent on others and may never move to the next level. When asking God for things we have to make sure that we are prepared for what we prayed for. God will keep us at stand still until he feels we are ready to level up.

"Sometimes God's blessing is not in what He gives; but in what He takes away. He knows best, trust Him."

Chapter 8

Becoming Whole-
♥ ♥ ♥ Know Your Self Worth ♥ ♥ ♥

    We have to learn that our circumstances don't define who we are but knowing our self-worth does. When I started putting up with disrespect from men, I was able to see the toxicity I had allowed in my life. As women we tend to look to men for love, but we have to first learn to love ourselves. We have to accept that everyone isn't going to give the same love we put out. I stopped taking things personally that people did or said to me. Love is now a feeling that I consider to be sacred and everyone doesn't deserve it from me. I didn't always think that way until I learned my love language which we'll speak on later in this book.

    As people we have to learn to love everything about ourselves even without a mate or people in general. I have been the type of person that tried to do all I could to prove to people I love, care, and support them only to get stabbed in the back. Now I know the meaning of true friendship, love, and support from genuine people. I'm not saying I'm perfect but I never been devious or malicious. Do I have a mean streak? Of course, I do and I won't make excuses about it. My upbringing was not the best as you have read, so it traumatized me to a sense as well as made me stronger. When I was a child, I was mean as hell with a lot of pent-up anger. However, as an adult, I have never been just flat-out mean unless something was brought to me. I didn't care about fighting or how big you were because we all bled the same. Then it came to a point where I have stuff to lose and children to raise. I avoided altercations best I could unless I had no choice. We have to remove ourselves from situations and people that could possibly make us act out.

    We as people have talked junk about someone at one point or another and if someone says they didn't their lying. Drama was something I was involved in not because I wanted to but because I chose those types of crowds. I use to

Tamika Melvin

get excited at the sound of gossip, beef, drama or someone else down falls.

The Naked Truth

Why? Because I wasn't happy with my own life. My priorities had to change and when they did none of that nonsense excited me anymore.

I had to get out my own way and pray that demon off me because as God's people we should never be happy at the expense of someone else hurt. I don't even get excited or want to be bothered to hear certain things no more. I was raised with sitting with the women in my family and gossip. It was always something going on between the family, especially the women. The gossip doesn't move me at all now but what it does is distance me from the person bringing the bones and deal with them differently.

If we want to get to a better level of self-worth, we have to stop entertaining toxic people and remove things that aren't good for our well-being. A healthy mindset will help you be productive and accomplish the goals you set for yourself. You will then stay on positive path and not become stagnant doing the same things over again. You have to walk and talk in the direction you want your life to go. I wanted to be a screenwriter and teach others how to write so I had to go back to school. Therefore, my attention had to be focused so I could reach my dreams. I enrolled in school and finished my last twenty-two credits within six months. I was extremely excited and even got a better gig with my writing. When we put our mind to it, we can do it but faith must be present.

Our mission should always be to reach a better version of ourselves. My priorities in life changed tremendously when I learned my self-worth. I was standing on something different and things that use to move me didn't anymore. We have to praise God at all times to keep a peaceful mind. People please know your self-worth because mine right now is higher and I demand way more than I use to.

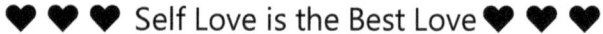

♥ ♥ ♥ Self Love is the Best Love ♥ ♥ ♥

First, I want to say you should always fall in love with you and love everything about yourself before loving someone else. If you can love yourself fully you have to have a period of time to be completely alone. You should never be at the mercy of others to be happy. People who are afraid to be alone tolerate people who shouldn't be in their life. They won't know the love of self if they just attach themselves to anyone for companionship. We have to stay away from people who attack us because they have issues.

I have always had the spirit of discernment. I can feel and know something was going to happen before it actually did. I began to ask God for revelation of who needed to be in my life and he did just that. I saw who was real and who was fake. I immediately started weeding out the people I saw bringing my energy down. I realized that energy grows where energy goes and if all you had to offer was drama, I cut it off immediately.

I am no longer that person who wanted to be involved in that mess. I removed others burdens because I used to live as if it were mine to bare. Closing that chapter and depending on myself helped me elevate to level I could have never imagine. I want my mind and body healthy so it was up to me to do so. I stopped smoking February 2021 cold turkey and it wasn't easy.

Our past can damage us if we don't let go, release, and heal. Healing was a great part of my process because I was broken in so many ways. I lost my Nana March 2019, my Mom July 2019, my father December 2020, and my grandfather who was my father figure June 2021. I felt like I lost two set of parents back-to-back. I was sleeping with a man I know I shouldn't have been dealing with at all. I needed time to grieve and I was doing it correctly. I was lost and full of grief and was headed in a downward spiral quickly.

I resented God because I felt like he was taking everyone I loved. Sometimes we have to be still and talk to God to heal ourselves. We have to trust and lean on him in our darkest hour. So, August 2020, I dedicated myself to learn to love God fully because I had limited experience with genuine love. I started attending morning prayer again and accepting the new dynamic of not having my mom or nana. I was broken because I was angry at God but he loved me enough to turn it all around. He healed me from inside out, neutralized my mind, and restored my soul. I became renewed that I saw the answers of my prayers unfold. Everything changed for the better for me from that point of dedication on. I was holding on to negative experiences that had me questioning my worthiness to be alive.

    I talked to God daily, prayed, meditated, exercised, and began yoga. We need to know that once we're healthy our mind is going to stay on a positive realm. Healthy lifestyles make us more productive, rested, happy, energized, and less stressed. I met my fiancée who showed me a healthier eating lifestyle and it's been the best for me physically. He cooks delicious nutritious meals that are low in fats and sugars. I eat less processed foods and now we're adopting a vegetarian lifestyle. Eating healthier and exercising makes us feel good about who we are. I'm learning to live now and not just cope in life like I have these last 43 years.

    My goal for this book The Naked Truth-Remember My Name is to show you no matter what the obstacles are you can do anything you put your mind to as long as you have faith and keep God first.

Thanks for sharing my journey
Tamika Melvin AKA
Lit Queen Meek

www.ingramcontent.com/pod-product-compliance
Ingram Content Group UK Ltd.
Pitfield, Milton Keynes, MK11 3LW, UK
UKHW041424180426
11947UKWH00007B/281